Title: What is Thanksgiving Day?

Author: Margot Parker

The story of the first thanksgiving in falsified. The actual facts are skewed to make light of a serious situation.

What Is Thanksgiving Day?

By Margot Parker

Illustrated by Matt Bates

CP CHILDRENS PRESS ®

CHICAGO

Library of Congress Cataloging-in-Publication Data

Parker, Margot.
  What is Thanksgiving Day? / by Margot Parker ; Matt Bates,
illustrator.
      p.   cm.
  Summary: Amy explains to Ben the origins of Thanksgiving Day.
  ISBN 0-516-03783-8
  1. Thanksgiving Day—Juvenile literature. [1. Thanksgiving Day.]
I. Bates, Matt, ill. II. Title.
GT4975.P37 1988   88-11112
394.2′683—dc19   CIP
                                                    AC

Childrens Press®, Chicago

"Ben," called Amy. "Please come in and help me."

"Amy, can't you see I'm busy?"
"Please, Ben! I want to make some

cookies for Thanksgiving Day."
"What is Thanksgiving Day?"

"It's when the Indians brought food for the Pilgrims."

"What is a Pilgrim?" asked Ben.

"Pilgrims were people who left England
so they would be free to worship God
in the way they wanted.

"Their ship was the *Mayflower*. It carried 102 people from England to America in the year 1620."

"Where is England?" asked Ben.
"It is far across the ocean," said

Amy. "For such a long trip, each family could take only their Bible, a chest for clothing, pots and pans for cooking, tools for building, and guns for hunting."

Amy continued, "At night, some families had to sleep on the deck of the ship."

"What did they eat," asked Ben?

"For two months they ate the same things day after day," said Amy.

"Salted beef or pork, fish caught from

the ocean, dried peas and beans, cheese, butter, and hardtack."

"Hardtack?" asked Ben.

"It was a hard, dry biscuit made of flour and water," explained Amy.

15

"The only way food could be cooked was in metal boxes. But most of the time the Pilgrims ate cold food.

"Many people were sick during the trip," continued Amy.

"Did they land safely?" asked Ben.

"Yes," said Amy. "On December 16, 1620, the *Mayflower* dropped anchor at what we now call Provincetown Harbor.

When the Pilgrims got off the ship, the first thing they did was to thank God for the safe journey.

"After that, the Pilgrims looked for a place to live. When they found the place, they named it Plymouth.

"The Pilgrims chopped down trees, trimmed them to make logs, and built a common house."

"Common house?" asked Ben. "What's that?"

"It was a large building that housed the men who worked and gave them a place to keep their tools," answered Amy.

"Later it was used as a church and hospital.

"The Pilgrims worked very hard that winter. Then in spring they met their first Indian friends.

"One of the first Indians they met was named Squanto.

"Squanto showed the Pilgrims new ways to fish and how to find wild plants that were good to eat.

"He also showed them how to plant corn. He planted the corn kernels on a little hill where he had buried three dead fish. As the fish decayed, they became fertilizer, and made the corn grow.

"That spring, on April 5, 1621, the *Mayflower* sailed back to England, leaving the Pilgrims behind in America.

"The Pilgrims liked their new land.
They built houses, worked on their
gardens, and hunted for food.

"In the summer the corn grew tall and there was plenty of food to eat. The Pilgrims knew that, if they were careful, no one would go hungry next winter.

"The Pilgrims had much to be thankful

for. The Indians had become their
friends and they had plenty of food.

"But, best of all, they had found a place to live where they could worship God in their own way.

"The Pilgrims decided to give thanks.
They set a time when no one had to
work, which they called Thanksgiving.

"The Pilgrims especially wanted to thank the Indians for the help they had given them. So they asked them to come to their Thanksgiving celebration.

"The first Thanksgiving lasted three days. All the Pilgrim families and their Indian friends came.

"Everyone brought something. The Pilgrim men brought ducks, geese, and fish.

"The Indians brought wild turkey, deer meat, and cookies," said Amy.

"The women served the meats with bread, nuts, and vegetables. Everyone ate outside on big tables.

"After dinner the Pilgrims and Indians played games and had contests to see who could run the fastest, throw a rock the farthest, or shoot an arrow the straightest.

"But most of the time at the
celebration was spent giving thanks
for the new land and new friends."

Amy's story was almost finished. She drew a deep breath. "So you see, Thanksgiving was a time for eating, playing, and sharing. But most of all, it was a time for giving thanks to God."

Ben was sorry that the story had ended. "Amy," he said, "that was a great story—especially the part about the Indians bringing cookies!"

"All right," said Amy, laughing. "You can be an Indian, and I'll be a Pilgrim. The cookies are out of the oven, so we can have our own special Thanksgiving."

Ben picked up a cookie and was all set to eat it when Amy said, "Not yet, Ben. First we must give thanks!"

44

And so Ben and Amy bowed their heads and thanked God for all the good things they had.

Then Ben took a large bite of cookie. "You know, Amy," he said, "I think cookies taste better when we remember to give thanks."

"Let's try to remember how important that is," said Amy. "Now hurry and finish your cookie so that we can go play some games!"

EPILOGUE

Congress ruled in 1941 that Thanksgiving would be a legal federal holiday observed the fourth Thursday in November. Canada celebrates Thanksgiving much the same as the United States. Their holiday is the second Monday in October.

THE AUTHOR

Margot Parker has been a kindergarten teacher with Sacramento City Schools for more than twenty years. She is a graduate of California State University at Sacramento, is married, and has two grown children. Her search for illustrated books that explain why people celebrate special days prompted her to write this *What Is* series for young children.

THE ILLUSTRATOR

Matt Bates studied art at Consumnes River College in Sacramento and the California Institute of the Arts in Valencia, where he studied under Walt Disney animators Hal Ambro and Bob McCrea, and designers T. Hee and Ray Aragon. Matt is currently working in the feature animation department at the Walt Disney Company